OBJECT LESSONS
WITH
EASY-TO-FIND OBJECTS

JESSIE P. SULLIVAN

BAKER BOOK HOUSE
Grand Rapids, Michigan 49506

ISBN: 0-8010-8190-4

Eleventh printing, April 1994

Printed in the United States of America

Contents

1 God Wants Us to "Call Him Up"!

Object: *Homemade telephone. (You will need two empty tin cans, each with one lid removed, and a string long enough to reach out of earshot. Punch a small hole in the center of the bottom of each can, thread the string through the hole to the inside, and knot the string securely. Choose a child to hold one can up to his ear while you go out of earshot with the other. Pull the string taut and speak into the can. Return to the child and ask him to repeat what he heard. Explain that the voice travels through the string from one can to the other.)*

Today nearly every home and business in the United States has a telephone. What could we possibly do without telephones?

If we want to chat with a friend, we simply call him

up. We can do this if our friend lives hundreds or even thousands of miles away in Israel or England.

The telephone is one of man's greatest inventions. But there is a phone greater than the one made by Alexander Graham Bell. This phone has what you might call a "hot line."

A hot line connects two phones that are always open and always kept available. The homemade phone you see here is like a hot line. The line goes directly from one station to another.

The very special hot line I am talking about today is one without a receiver, wires, or a dial. It is the one that is connected to God!

It doesn't make any difference where you are or what you are doing. Your hot line to God is always open! God is always available and waiting to hear your message.

This hot line to God is called "prayer." We can use it to ask for help, to praise God, and to thank Him for everything He has done for us, especially for sending His Son Jesus into the world so we can have eternal life.

Would you like to use your hot line to God to tell Him you love Him and want to accept Jesus as your Savior? If you do, He answers you by saying, "But as many as received Him, to them gave He power to become the sons of God, even to them that believe on His name" (John 1:12).

2 The Book of Life

Object: *Telephone book.*

(Hold up the telephone book.) This book has many names in it. It probably has your father's or mother's and maybe even your grandparents' names. Some day if you have a telephone your name will probably be in a telephone book.

Do you know that there is a book in heaven that is much, much bigger than this? It is called the Book of Life, and in it is the name of every person who has accepted Jesus as his or her Savior. It even has the names of all the boys and girls who have accepted Jesus!

Some day every one whose name is in the Book of Life will be in heaven with God. Is your name written in God's Book of Life? If it isn't, would you like to know how to have it there?

The first thing you need to do is to admit that you have done things that are displeasing to God. The Bible says that "all have sinned, and come short of the glory of God" (Rom. 3:23).

You yourself cannot do anything about your sins, even though the wages of sin is death. What you *can* do is to accept the gift that God has given you, His Son Jesus Christ. "The wages of sin is death; but the gift of God is eternal life through Jesus Christ our Lord" (Rom. 6:23)

Christ died on the cross for your sins. If you repent and accept what He has done for you, you can have eternal life. Then you can be sure your name is in the Book of Life.

3 God Protects Us

Object: *A pair of rubber boots.*

If we let God come into our lives, He will always take care of us. He knows what is best for each of us. God also knows all about us. He even knew us before we were born! He knows our futures, too.

Because we can never know all the things God knows about us, we should be grateful and happy that He knows what is best for us and sees that we get it. The Bible says, "Rejoice evermore. Pray without ceasing. In every thing give thanks: for this is the will of God in Christ Jesus concerning you" (I Thess. 5:16-18).

When it rains or snows, most mothers see to it that their children put their rubber boots on before they go out so they won't get their feet cold and wet. (Show boots.)

Have you ever gone out without your boots when your mother told you to wear them? If you have, you probably got your feet all wet and muddy, and found out that your mother knew what was best. She knew because she is older and wiser than you are. God gave us mothers and fathers so they could help Him take care of us.

Just think. If your mother knows all these things that help you, how much more God must know!

Isn't it good to know that God, who knows everything there is to know, loves us and takes care of us?

4 A Life for Life

Object: *A fruit seed or a package of flower seeds.*

It is hard to understand why Jesus had to come to earth and die for us before we could become God's children. Perhaps this seed will help us to understand. (Show seed.)

If you buried this seed in the ground, what could you expect? The buried seed will lie there for a while. After you have watered it and the sunshine has warmed the soil, something very marvelous will begin to happen. A tiny green sprout will start to peek out of the ground. This little sprout begins to push up, up, up, until it becomes a plant.

We can watch the plant grow after it comes out of the ground. But what has happened down under the ground before you could see that plant? The seed died. It had to die in order to give life.

And that is the way it was with Jesus. He had to die so we could have eternal life.

God is a holy God. Everyone falls short of God's glory because everyone has sinned by doing things that displease God. Have you ever lied or taken something that did not belong to you? Cheated in school or disobeyed your parents?

God provided a way for you to be able to have a new life and live with Him forever, even though you have done some of these things. That way is Jesus.

When Jesus came to the earth, He came so He could give us eternal life. But first He had to die. "For God so loved the world, that He gave His only begotten Son, that whosoever believeth in Him should not perish, but have everlasting life" (John 3:16).

God loves us very much, and He wants each one of us to live with Him forever.

5 Power from God

Object: *Electric toothbrush.*

Some dentists say that if you always clean your teeth properly you will never have any cavities! There is one dentist whose three children have never had a cavity! He says that is because their teeth have always been cleaned properly. He also says that an electric toothbrush is good to use because it cleans your teeth better than a regular toothbrush and massages your gums.

This is an electric toothbrush. (Show brush.) As you can see, the handle of the brush has a cord in it. The cord has a place on the end of it where it can be plugged into an electrical outlet.

Will this toothbrush do much good as it is now? No, you have to plug the cord into an electric circuit for power before it can do what it is supposed to do. That is the way it is with people, too. We cannot have power unless we connect ourselves up with the power of God. We can do this by accepting His Son Jesus Christ as our Lord and Savior and allowing Him to come into our lives. God is always ready to receive us. He waits for each one of us to come to Him so He can fill us with His power.

6 Your Journey Through Life

Object: *Suitcase with large cards in it. Each card should have a different word printed on it, such as Bible, Prayer, Faith, Love, Obedience. It is good to have a few blank cards on hand in case a child has an idea you want to add.*

Everybody likes to travel. Some people like to travel to big cities where it is noisy and there are many things to do. Others like to go out into the country where it is quiet and peaceful. Some people travel a long, long way from home; others never travel very far. But everybody makes at least one trip—the trip through life!

When we go on a trip, we pack things to take along. This suitcase (show it) has in it some of the things we can take along with us as we make our journey through life. Let's look at the objects in our suitcase and see how they will help us on our journey. (Open the suitcase. Let the children draw the cards out one by one.)

Bible: We need the Bible to know what we are supposed to do and where we are supposed to go. The Bible tells us to accept Jesus as our Savior.

Faith: Without faith in God we are going in the wrong direction. We need faith in Him to lead us the right way. Faith is the map we need to follow on our trip.

Prayer: We need to talk to God all the time. We pray so we can find out what He wants us to do in our lives. He provides directions for our trip.

Love: God tells us to love Him more than anything

in the whole world. He also tells us to love ourselves and everybody else. If we follow God's commandment to love, we will make Him and ourselves happy. Love helps us enjoy our trip.

Obedience: When we read the Bible, we find out what God wants us to do. The Bible says to obey our parents, to be kind, to be forgiving, and many other things.

As you travel through life, what are you going to pack in your suitcase?

3\96

7 Going God's Way

Object: *A road map.*

Have you ever gone for a ride with someone and gotten lost? Sometimes when this happens the driver will drive all around in search of his destination. Or he might ask somebody along the road for directions. But the person he asks might not know how to get there either, or he might know but might not give the directions correctly. The driver sometimes gets so discouraged that he turns around and goes home, leaving everyone disappointed.

The best thing to do if you don't know how to get some place is to get a map of the area you are interested in. This map (show map) is a plan of _____ (name city or state). It is a diagram of _____ (city or state).

If you were looking for a certain place, you could find

where it is on the map and figure out how to get there without much trouble.

Do you know that God has a plan for your life? He knew the direction He wanted you to take even before you were born. He made you as you are so you could go where He wants you to go. God doesn't show you where He wants you to go all at once, though. He leads you step by step, day by day.

If you want to follow God's plan, you must listen to Him all the time so you will know His plan. If you let Him lead you each step of the way, He will direct you through your entire life.

God knows what is best and right for us. If we follow Him, we will reach the destination He planned for us long ago. And, because God loves us, we know the life He planned for us is one of happiness and abundance.

8 Inside, Outside

Object: *Mirror*

What do you see when you look into this mirror? You see yourself! At least, you see how you look on the *outside*.

A mirror shows you what other people see when they look at you. But God does not look at you as other people do; He not only sees you on the *outside*, but also on the *inside*!

Others can see, like the mirror, if your hair is combed and if your face is clean. But God can see if your thoughts are good and clean. He can see how you feel, too. God knows all about you.

If God knows all about you, why do you suppose He tells you to talk to Him? He must have a reason. Do you suppose it is because He wants to talk with us because He loves us? Or, is it because we will love Him more if we talk to Him? Maybe it is because when we see He has answered our prayers we are more thankful for what He does for us.

When we pray we must believe God will do what He says He will do. We are to be forgiving. Jesus told His disciples in Mark 11:25 that they were to forgive anybody they had a grudge against. "Then," Jesus said, "you can pray for anything, and if you believe, you have it; it's yours!"

Most importantly, we should ask God to forgive our sins. Then we can thank Jesus for being our Savior.

God knows when we are truly sorry for our sins and if we really love Jesus. But even though He already knows it, He wants us to *say* it. He wants us to confess it with our mouths.

9 Jesus Washes Away Our Sins

Objects: *Shampoo and basin.*

Do you ever wash your hair? How do you do it? You get your hair wet and put shampoo on it. (Show shampoo.) Then you rub and rub until you get lots of lather. Finally you put your hair under water (show basin) and wash all the suds out. Sometimes you have to do this several times before you get your hair clean, but after you are through and your hair is dry, it is shiny and pretty and it smells good!

If you wanted to wash your hair, would it do any good just to look at the shampoo? No, you have to get your hair wet, apply shampoo, and rub and rub until you get suds. Then you have to wash the suds out.

Jesus is a bit like shampoo. Many people have heard about Jesus. Many people come to church. Many have even read the Bible. But even if you have done all these things, it does not do any good if you have not done the most important thing of all. You have to take Jesus out of the Bible and make Him your own. You have to apply Him to your life and let Him be your Savior.

When you see yourself as God sees you, and when you realize how many things you have done that make God unhappy, ask Him to forgive you. That is like getting your hair wet before a shampoo. Then accept Jesus and He will wash away all your sins.

God sent Jesus to the earth to be an example for us and to tell us about God's kingdom. When He died on the cross, He took all our sins upon Himself. When He arose from the grave, He overcame death. That is why we can have eternal life.

Jesus did everything for us. All we have to do is to repent of our sins and accept Him.

10 Coals of Fire

Object: *Lump of coal, or a log.*

The Bible says, "If your enemy is hungry, feed him; if he is thirsty, give him to drink; for by doing this you will heap burning coals on his head" (Rom. 12:20).

Heaping coals of fire on someone's head sounds like a very cruel thing to do, but it wasn't in Jesus' time. Back then no one had matches, so they had to keep their fires burning in the fireplace all the time. Sometimes, though, someone would get careless and let his fire go out. Since there was no way to relight the fire, somebody would have to go to a neighbor's house for some hot, live coals to start the fire again.

These coals were carried in a container perched on the person's head. So, heaping burning coals on someone's head was actually an act of kindness! It was giving the person the opportunity to have hot food and water and to be warm when it was cold outside.

We don't help people by giving them hot coals or logs (show lump of coal or log) today because we have automatic pilot lights, electricity, and matches. So, if you wanted to do something kind for somebody who did not like you, what could you do?

You could share some of your candy or gum with him. Perhaps you could invite him to your house to play, or invite him to come to Sunday school and church with you. At least you could say kind things to him.

If you are mean and unkind, other people will think that Jesus is mean and unkind. They will not listen if you try to tell them about Jesus. If you are forgiving and kind, people will see that Jesus is forgiving and kind. They will see Jesus in you. You will feel good about yourself and others and you'll want to tell them about Jesus, and they will listen.

11 We Can Depend upon God

Object: *Safety pin.*

A safety pin is a very handy object when you need to hold something together. When you are away from home and a button comes off your shirt or blouse, or the hem comes out of your pant leg or dress, you are glad to have a safety pin.

But have you ever thought of this? That safety pin would not do one bit of good if it weren't dependable, or didn't do what it was supposed to do. If that pin kept coming undone, it not only wouldn't be dependable, it would be dangerous! If you have ever been stuck by a pin, you understand what I mean!

When a person is dependable, he does what he is supposed to do. He is dependable if he is always on time at school or Sunday school and if he does the work assigned him. A dependable person also keeps secrets and tells the truth.

God wants us to be dependable. He wants us to keep our promises.

We know God always keeps His promises. He promised to send His Son Jesus to the earth to save us from our sins. And He did send Jesus. But we decide whether or not we want to accept Jesus as our Savior.

It's good to know we are always able to depend on God.

12 A Replica of Jesus

Objects: *Two pieces of clean paper, a piece of carbon paper, a pencil.*

Have you ever made a carbon copy of anything? (If there is a child who hasn't, ask him to draw something for you on the top clean sheet, putting the carbon between it and the bottom sheet of paper. If everyone has made a carbon, select anyone to demonstrate. After the child draws on the paper, show the results.)

A carbon copy looks like the original and is called a replica. A replica looks like the master copy, but, as you see here, it is not the master copy.

When you know Jesus as your Savior, He becomes not only your Savior, but your Master. You should read the Bible every day to find out what it says about Jesus. Then, knowing how and why He did the things He did, and knowing what He said, you can be a replica, or copy, of Him.

But you cannot be a replica of Jesus without His help. You must ask God to help you understand what He says to you in the Bible. You also need to ask Him to forgive you for the wrong things you have done and for the bad thoughts you have thought. If you ask Him to forgive you, He will.

The more we read God's Word, the Bible, and let God talk to us, the more we will know about Him. The more we pray and do what He says, the more like Jesus we will be.

Won't it be wonderful when someone can look at us and say, "You must belong to Jesus, because you act just like Him"?

13 Hang Your Life on Jesus

Object: *A coat hanger.*

When Mary comes home from school every afternoon, she changes her clothes. After she takes off her school dress and puts on her play clothes, she hangs her dress on a hanger and places it in the closet. (Show hanger.) By doing this Mary can sometimes wear the same clothes to school several days before they are dirty and have to be put into the dirty-clothes basket.

But in order for Mary to keep her clean clothes from being messed up, she has to take the time and the energy to get a hanger out of her closet, put her dress on it, and hang it up.

If you want to keep your life in good order, you have to do something, too. You have to hang your life on Jesus and keep it there!

The trouble is that sometimes Christians, people who accept Jesus as their Savior, don't want to live for Him. The Bible teaches that when we accept Jesus as our Lord and personal Savior we are saved forever. God has given us the gift of life and He will never take that gift away.

However, sometimes we forget we belong to Jesus and do things that displease Him. When we do, we should immediately ask God to forgive us and give ourselves back to Him.

God is always ready to forgive us. And when we ask Him to take our lives over again, it is like picking up a garment, pressing it, and hanging it on a hanger.

When you see a hanger, let it remind you of Jesus and how He is always ready and willing to accept you when you are ready and willing to accept Him.

14 A Living Branch

Object: *A tree branch, preferably one with leaves.*

See this branch? (Show branch.) It came from a tree. Before it was broken off, it was an important part of the tree, and the tree was very important to the branch. In fact, that tree was so important to this branch that it gave the branch life. As long as it was a part of the tree, it received the nourishing sap that flowed in that tree's trunk and gave the branch life.

Now the branch will die and become dry and hard. It will no longer bear leaves, and the leaves that are on it will die and fall off. Perhaps it won't be entirely useless, because I could use it to burn in a fireplace; or, if it were big enough, I could make a board out of it. But its life is gone. It is no longer valuable as far as the trunk is concerned.

That's the way it is with Jesus and Christians. When a person accepts Jesus as his Savior from sin, he becomes like a branch. As long as that person remains attached and submitted to Jesus, he is a vital living part of Jesus.

But a person who breaks away from Jesus after becoming a part of Him, will suffer. He will wither away because he has not stayed close to Jesus, who gave him life. Jesus goes on living and doing what God wants Him to do, but the Christian's witness withers away and he becomes unhappy. He is still a Christian, just as the branch is still wood, but his growth and vitality are gone.

A tree branch can't reattach itself to a tree, but a Christian can ask God to forgive him and reattach himself to Christ's life. If you want to be closer to Jesus, you should think about what it is in your life that keeps you from being close to Him. Do you have a bad temper, or do you complain a lot? Ask God to forgive you of your sins, and to take over your life again.

Nobody wants to be a withered old Christian when he can be a vital, effective one!

15 Why We Have the Lord's Supper

Objects: *Tray with unleavened bread and cup of wine or grape juice used in communion services.*

Many of you have been in the adult church and have seen your parents participate in a ceremony which they call the Lord's Supper, or Communion. Men who are chosen by the church pass around a dish and a tray of wine or grape juice. People take a piece of bread from the dish and a little glass from the tray when it is passed to them. Sometimes the wine (grape juice) is in a large cup from which they all drink.

In most churches (explain here how your church observes the Lord's Supper), only those people who have accepted Jesus as their Savior are supposed to take any of the bread or wine. This is because Communion is a special ceremony which Jesus Himself started in order that we might do something to help us remember all He has done for us.

After you become old enough to understand what it is to be a sinner in need of a Savior and after you have accepted Jesus as that Savior, then you may have the privilege of taking some of the bread and wine (grape juice).

The bread represents Jesus' body which He gave for us. The wine represents the blood which He shed for us. When we eat the bread which represents Jesus' body and drink the wine which represents His blood, we should be very reverent. It is a time to think about God and Jesus and all He has done for us. It is a time to be very quiet and prayerful and to thank God for His great gift, His Son, Jesus Christ.

16 God Knows What Is Best

Object: *Medicine.*

God wants us to be obedient. In the Bible He tells children to obey their parents and everyone to obey the government. But, above all, He wants everyone to be obedient to Him. He knows that it is for our own good for us to learn to be obedient.

Have you ever been sick and gone to the doctor? If you have, the doctor probably gave you some medicine to take. Maybe he gave you something like this. (Show medicine.) He gave you the medicine because he thought it would make you well again. But the only way the medicine can help you is to take it!

Learning to be obedient is important for boys and girls because it helps them to learn to do the right things at the right time. If you grow up having your own way all the time, you will end up in trouble with your parents, with your government, and even with God. You will never be happy.

Jesus was always obedient to God. He came to earth and lived as a man because God wanted Him to. God wanted Him to live a perfect life and to die for the sins of all mankind. If Jesus had not been obedient, we would not go to heaven when we die. We would not be able to have eternal life.

I am glad Jesus was obedient to God. Do you want to be obedient to Him, too?

17 God's Gift

Object: *Spot remover.*

When you get a spot on your clothes, sometimes you can wash it out with soap and water. But sometimes soap and water doesn't work. You might need to use something special like this spot remover. (Show remover.)

God, who is holy, cannot look at anything that is not perfect. He cannot look at the big dark spots in our lives that are not clean and pure. Everyone in the whole world has this problem because "all have sinned, and come short of the glory of God" (Rom. 3:23).

This puts us in a pretty bad position, doesn't it? If we are sinners and God can't look at us, how can we ever be with Him in heaven?

God gave us a solution. He sent Someone who does more than remove our bad spots of sin. He sent Jesus to die on the cross to take our punishment so His blood could completely remove and cover our sins. Because of Jesus, we can be holy and pure and clean and new to live with God forever.

God has given us Jesus and salvation as a free gift. We don't have to do anything but be sorry for our sins and accept His gift. To do this we say in our hearts, "Forgive me of my sins, God. I accept what Jesus and You have done for me. Thank You for my salvation."

18 God Loves Us

Objects: *Blanket and chair.*

When Jesus died on the cross, He gave His life for you and me. He didn't have to do it. He did it because He loves us. His love is much, much greater than any other love in the whole world.

God loved us so much that while we were still sinners He let His only Son die for us. He loved us in spite of the fact that we did things that were bad, like cheating, lying, and hurting other people. He loved us in spite of the fact that we didn't even like Him!

But do you know what happened when Jesus died for us? It was just like this. (Open blanket.) See this chair? Pretend it represents all the bad things you ever did. (Cover the chair with the blanket.)

When Jesus died, His blood covered all your sins as if they had never existed. Our sins are all washed away, covered just like this chair is covered. We become God's children when we accept Jesus as our Savior. We are no longer separated from God.

Just as the blanket completely covers this chair, Jesus' blood completely covers our sins.

19 We Are like Salt

Object: *A box of salt.*

Salt is so common to us that we really don't think about it much; but if we didn't have it, we would miss it very much.

Salt does a lot of things. First, it is a seasoner. Have you ever tasted mashed potatoes that didn't have any salt in them? If you have, you know how flat and tasteless they are. Just a little salt makes them taste very good.

Most food is like that. It tastes dull and flat with no seasoning; but when you put seasoning on it, it becomes good and tasty.

Salt is also a preserver. When some foods are treated with salt, they last a long time without refrigeration.

Salt can melt ice if you put it out on your icy side-walk or driveway on a cold, winter day.

Salt is a purifier, too. It kills germs.

Did you know that Jesus tells us in Matthew that Christians are supposed to be the salt of the earth?

How can we be the salt of the earth? By being warm and friendly to other people. By being the kind of people they like to be around so they can see the love of Jesus in our lives.

Salt isn't any good unless it is used, and so it is with us. We should make an effort to be with people and let them know about Jesus. We should be so pleasant to be around that they want to know what it is that makes us that way. As we live a Christian life obedient to God and His commandments and honoring Him at all times, we'll be able to talk to others about Jesus. We will be able to tell them that if they accept Jesus as their Savior, they, too, can be the salt of the earth!

20 God Wants to Use Us

Object: *Salt shaker.*

God has a plan for each of us. In fact, God knew before He ever created the world exactly what He wanted you to look like, who your parents would be, and what He would like you to do with your life!

God's plans are always right because He knows everything. God loves us and wants what is best for us.

But sometimes we do the wrong things because we haven't tried to find out what God wants us to do, or because we don't have enough self-discipline to do what is right. Sometimes we are just too stubborn to do what God wants us to do.

Take this salt shaker, for example. (Show shaker.) It was made for a purpose. It is the right size for a salt shaker. It has holes in the top so it can be used as a salt shaker and it even has salt in it. But it really doesn't function as a salt shaker unless I use it.

What if I were eating dinner and I needed some salt, reached over for the salt shaker to put some on my potatoes, and couldn't pick it up? (Act as if you are trying very hard to pick the shaker up, but can't.) It doesn't make any difference how hard I try; if the salt shaker refuses to let me lift it up, my potatoes will have to go unsalted.

God has made you for a purpose, just as this salt shaker was made for a purpose. If you want to let God use you, you must read the Bible and see what He wants you to do. You must pray and listen to what He tells you. And you must be obedient and do it.

Just remember. God wants you to be obedient to Him so He can make your life happy and abundant. God loves you. You don't ever have to worry about what He wants for you. He wants only the best!

21 We Need to Be "Connected" to Have Power

Object: *Light bulb.*

(Show light bulb.) Can somebody tell me what this is? (Allow someone to answer.) What is this light bulb supposed to do? (Allow someone to answer.) If this light bulb is supposed to shine, why isn't it shining? (Allow someone to answer.) That's right. It has to have electricity connected to it so the electricity can get into the bulb and give it the power to shine.

I'd like to have you pretend this light bulb is a person. This person goes about his daily life full of darkness. He looks around and sees other people who have something he doesn't have. "I'd like to have what those people have," he might think. "I'd like to have something in me that can give me the things they have. I want to be happy and to shine as they shine."

Imagine that one of these people comes up to our unlighted friend (point to the light bulb) and tells him about Jesus. And just suppose our unlighted friend accepts Jesus as his Savior. The very minute he accepts Jesus, something happens to him. The Holy Spirit comes into his heart.

If we could see the Holy Spirit come into his heart and life, he might look like this light bulb when it is connected to an electric socket. The electricity is the power that makes the light bulb shine when we turn it on.

29

When the Holy Spirit comes into our lives, we have power, too. We have the same power in us that raised Jesus from the dead. That's a lot of power, isn't it?

22 Lying Grows

Object: *A cake of yeast, or a package of dry yeast.*

Have you ever watched someone bake a loaf of bread, or some rolls? If you have, you've seen them put yeast in the dough. (Show yeast.)

After the dough is mixed, the baker lets it sit in a warm place for an hour or so. During that hour something strange and mysterious happens. The dough grows larger and larger. In fact, by the time the hour is up, the dough is twice as big as it had been an hour before!

There's something about yeast that makes the dough grow. But if you hadn't put it in the dough, the yeast itself wouldn't have grown at all.

Telling a lie is like putting yeast into dough. When you tell a lie, sometimes it doesn't seem very bad. In fact, it might even seem all right. And when you tell it, you might even think that's going to be all there is to it.

But, as I said before, a lie is a little like yeast, because once it is said, it seems to grow and grow. The first thing you know, you have to tell another lie to cover up the first one. And another one to cover up that one. One lie follows another until you get so confused you can't remember all the false things you've said!

God hates lying for God is Truth. If you want to be like Him, you will always tell the truth.

23 Eggs Have Shells

Objects: *A raw egg and a dish.*

There are many ways to prepare eggs. You can put a whole egg, shell and all, into water and let the water boil to make a boiled egg. If you want a hard-boiled egg, you boil the water for fifteen or twenty minutes. If you want a soft-boiled egg, you boil the water for just a few minutes.

Or, you can crack the shell and let the raw egg inside come out. (Crack shell and put the egg into the dish.) You can use this egg in many ways. You can use it in a cake, ice cream, or pudding. Or you can fry it and put salt and pepper on it. You can also put salt, pepper, milk, and butter with it, mix it all up, and fry it to make a scrambled egg.

Eggs also help the other ingredients stick together when you put them in cookies and cakes.

We already know that if you want to use an egg, you have to break the shell. What if the shell were so hard you couldn't break it? You wouldn't be able to use the egg, would you?

That's the way it sometimes is with people when God wants them to do something. They don't listen to Him, so they don't know what He wants. Some people do know what God wants and still don't do it. They are hard and stubborn—like an egg whose shell is so hard you can't break it.

God wants us to read the Bible and do what it says. He wants us to listen to Him and to do what He tells us to do. When we do what God says, He always blesses us.

Let's not be stubborn and hard. Let's let God use us so we may receive all the blessings He has for us.

24 Separated from the World

Object: *Egg separator. (If you don't have an egg separator, you can separate an egg into two cups.)*

(Show egg separator.) Some of you may not know what this is. It is an egg separator. It is used to separate the whites of an egg from the yolk.

Why does anyone need an egg separator? Some recipes call for just the yolks or just the whites of eggs.

If the recipe for a cake calls for only the whites of eggs, the cake will be white. If it calls for both the whites and the yolks, the cake will be yellow. If the recipe calls for only the yolks, the cake will be a deep yellow, almost orange.

Have you ever seen an angel food cake? If you have, you know it is white. If the cook didn't separate the yolks from the whites, she would not have a cake that was so nice, fluffy, and white.

God tells us to be separated from the world. If we are, we can be close to Him and we will be able to know His will in our lives.

But how can we be separated from the world, when we are in it? By separating ourselves from the things of Satan, who is the prince of the world. By staying away from the things we know are evil and wrong. And by not playing with other children who do bad things. By staying away from them we are able to do what God wants us to do.

Of course, we'll come in contact with bad things all the time. But we must learn to recognize and to turn away from them.

Can you name some of the things boys and girls should be very careful about if they want to be separated from the world? (After the children are allowed to name some worldly things, have prayer, asking God to show them all the things He wants them to stay away from. Ask Him to give them the discipline to be obedient to Him.)

25 God Wants Us to Love Each Other

Object: *Tube of glue.*

Have you ever tried to glue something together that just wouldn't stick? (Show tube of glue.) It can be very discouraging and even make you angry. Sometimes you work and work at it and it still falls apart. You try adding more glue and holding the two pieces together very tightly. Then, when you let go, and it still doesn't work, you just don't know what to do.

Did you know that Christians are supposed to stick together? We do that if we love one another. One of the most important tests to determine if you are a Christian is whether or not you love your fellow Christians. This love that Christians have for each other is like glue. It holds us together.

God says in Ephesians that Christians are living stones in the temple of God. He means that all Christians have a definite part in God's kingdom right here on earth. Each has a particular function to perform.

When everybody does his job right, God's work will prosper on earth. Besides doing our particular job, we must do something else, too. Remember the glue? We must stick together! Just think what a problem it would create in the church if we didn't do that.

Christian love is the glue that holds Christians together. It is what gives them unity. The church can't do a good job if people don't love each other. All of them would be spending their time trying to make the church fall down because they wouldn't be cooperating or working together.

You can also see how every single stone is important. If even one person is out of sorts with his fellow Christians, the building will begin to lean. In fact, I think one stone, or one Christian in a church, could keep Christ's work from going out into the community.

What kind of a Christian are you? Are you one who is filled with love for all your fellow Christians? If you are, you fit properly in your church! If you aren't, pray and ask God to forgive you for your lack of love. Then ask God to fill you with His love.

26 God Wants the Best for You

Object: *A sieve.*

Cooks use a sieve when they want to drain excess juice or water off something. (Show sieve.) Spaghetti, for instance. After the spaghetti boils in water until it is done, you have to pour off the hot water so the spaghetti won't get mushy and overcooked.

The water goes right through these little holes. The spaghetti doesn't because it is too big. After all the water drains through and only the spaghetti is left, the cook can use the spaghetti in any way he wants. He can put butter on it, or cheese, or sauce.

God is like a sieve because He can strain off the sin in our lives. One of the sins or bad things in our lives is bad attitudes—looking at everything in a negative way. Did you know that when you fuss and complain you are showing that you don't believe God? God says to thank Him for everything!

Another bad thing in our lives can be jealousy, or wishing we had something that belongs to somebody else. God hates laziness and lying, too.

In fact, there are a lot of things God hates. I'm sure you know a lot more. Maybe you even have some of these things in your life. If you do, ask God to remind you when you do something wrong and to help you stop doing it.

Let God strain off the sin in your life. Read your Bible and listen to God when you pray. He will tell you what He wants you to do, just as He'll tell you what He doesn't want you to do.

You will be a much happier person when you do what God wants you to do, because He loves you and wants only the best for you.

27 Make a Joyful Noise

Objects: *A pan and a spoon.*

(Bang the spoon against the pan, making as much noise as possible. Be sure you are smiling while you do this.)

What am I doing? (Allow the children to answer, guiding them to the right answer—"making a joyful noise.")

The Bible says to make a joyful noise unto the Lord. How can we do that? I made a joyful noise by beating this spoon against this pan. How can I make that noise to the Lord joyful? By thinking about how great and wonderful God is. By thinking about all the good things He has given us and by loving Him because He loves us so much. When we do this, we are worshiping God.

You can praise God by making a joyful noise right here where you sit. Can you name some ways? (Let the children name some ways they can make a joyful noise, like clapping, whistling, knocking on their chairs with their knuckles, etc.)

That seems very strange, but that's what God says. What He really wants us to do while we are making a joyful noise is to worship Him, love Him, and think about how wonderful He is.

I'd like each of you to select one of these ways to praise God. We will now praise Him together. But first, remember to think about God and His wonder while you do it, or it will be just noise.

(You worship God by beating on the pan with the spoon as each child worships in his own way. You may want the children to state beforehand how they will worship God. After a brief period, stop making noise and wait with bowed head until everyone has stopped. Now ask everyone to bow his head and close his eyes as you lead in a prayer praising God and thanking Him for all His blessings, including the opportunity to release ourselves in true worship.)

28 Practice Is Important

Object: *A ball.*

Playing ball is fun. People have so much fun playing ball they even like to watch other people play it!

No one ever got good at playing any kind of ball, whether it be baseball, volleyball, or football, without practicing.

Of course, some people find that they are naturally better at playing ball than other people. But even those who have a natural talent know that they won't ever be a good ballplayer unless they work at it. They have to practice and practice. The more they practice, the better they get.

In fact, even if you aren't especially talented, if you work hard at it, you can become better than you would be otherwise. In fact, you might get better than someone who is talented and never practices.

If you know God wants you to do something, work at it, and, with God's help, you'll be able to do it. God doesn't promise us a life of ease. But He does promise to help us. If you have a problem, ask God for help. Pray to Him if you don't know if you are doing what is right. He will show you the way.

For instance, God wants us to be forgiving. Do you find it hard to forgive people when you think they've done something to hurt you? If you do, ask God to help you and start practicing. Yes, practice forgiving people!

Forgiving others is like playing ball—the more you do it, the easier it becomes. It may be very hard at first, but don't give up. Keep working at it, and some day it will be easy for you.

29 Part of My Life

Object: *A dollar bill.*

(Hold bill up.) Do you see this dollar bill? It is part of me. Can someone tell me why? (Allow children time to answer.) It is part of me because I gave part of my life for it. I gave my time and energy to earn this dollar bill.

When I give this money to God, I am giving part of myself. As a matter of fact, when I stand up here and talk to you, I am giving you part of myself! I am giving you my time and energy.

Many people have the funny idea that when they give time, energy, and money to God, they are sacrificing, or giving up something. But giving to God is not a sacrifice. It is a seed planted.

There is a Bible verse that says, "Cast your bread upon the waters and it will not return unto you void."

This verse means that when you give something, it will come back to you bigger and better than when you gave it. It may not come back in the same form, but you'll receive a special blessing because of it. That is, if you have given something good.

Have you ever planted a vegetable seed and watched a plant grow from it? The plant grows many vegetables on it, and it also produces more seeds. But if that first seed had not been planted, no other seeds would have grown.

It's like that with my life, too. When I give God this dollar which is part of my life, I am sowing seed. God will use it to grow something for His kingdom. And besides helping God's kingdom, the money will help me, too, because God will multiply it back to me.

39

Today I'm planting the seed of my life in God's kingdom when I put this dollar in the offering plate. I'm giving it to God. I'm giving a part of myself to God. I'll trust Him to use it.

30 God's Timing Is Right

Object: *Clock.*

You may be too young to use an alarm clock, but if you don't use one your mother or father probably does.

Every night before I go to bed I set my alarm clock. (Show clock.) I set it at 6:30 in the morning because that's the time I need to get up so I can get to my job on time.

Every morning my faithful alarm clock rings at exactly the time I set it for. (Let alarm ring.) Because my alarm goes off at the right time I am able to get up, eat breakfast, and get ready to go to work.

God doesn't need an alarm clock, because He is always awake! And He knows everything, including the time when it is exactly right for things to happen.

Sometimes we try to push God to hurry Him and make things happen when we want them to. When we pray and ask God for something, we should pray believing He will answer us. But let's learn to be patient and wait for Him and His time. He knows when it is the best time for our prayers to be answered.

I am glad God knows everything, and that He loves us and knows what is best for us. Aren't you?

31 God Is Trustworthy

Object: *A potholder.*

The Bible tells us to trust God. Is there somebody here who can tell us what "trust" means? Can somebody give an example of trust?

(After discussion, display potholder.) When you want to take something out of a hot oven, you never take it out with your bare hands. If you did, you would burn yourself.

You use a potholder so your skin doesn't touch the hot pan or dish. You trust the potholder to protect you so you won't get burned. And, because you trust it, you use it.

But a potholder can't always be trusted. If it is too thin or wet, it won't protect you properly and you will get burned.

You can't always trust people, either, because sometimes they are unable to keep a promise. They might get sick, have an accident, or forget. Or they might not think it important to keep their word.

The Bible tells us the many promises God has given us. Many of those promises have already been kept. Many are still in the future. We can always trust God. He never forgets and He always keeps His promises.

Can Serve God

Object: *A bottle opener.*

Bottle Opener lay quietly in the kitchen drawer. In fact, according to Bottle Opener, he lay *too* quietly. He never got to do anything!

Bottle Opener noticed that Can Opener got to perform often. Their mistress would come to the drawer and shift all the utensils around. Each time she did, Bottle Opener held his breath. Would he get to do something for his mistress this time? He dearly loved the lady who used the articles in the drawer. He sincerely wished he could get to do more for her. But she rarely chose him to do any of her jobs.

What made it so bad was that the mistress used all the other utensils often. Not only did she use Can Opener, but nearly every day she used Spatula and Cooking Fork. And, as for the Tablespoons, even though there were many of them, they got to serve over and over again.

"I wish I were something else," Bottle Opener said to himself one day when he felt especially depressed. He felt so depressed that when the mistress shuffled everything around in the drawer he let himself be pushed way over in a corner out of sight. Bottle Opener moped all day. "Nobody wants me," he said to himself. "I'm just not good for anything."

Then it happened. Bottle Opener didn't even have to blink his eyes when the drawer opened because he was so far back in the corner, but he could hear the mistress talking. "Where, oh, where is my Bottle Opener," she said. "I was sure it was here. I see it all the time when

I'm getting something else from the drawer. Why can't I see it now?"

Was it true? Did the mistress really want to use him? Bottle Opener tried and tried to make himself conspicuous, but the mistress didn't see him.

Finally she said, "I guess I'll just have to dump everything out of the drawer. Nothing can substitute for the Bottle Opener. It has a very special job to do."

Nothing could substitute for him? Could nothing take his place? Bottle Opener began to get excited. When the mistress dumped the things out of the drawer, he managed to land on top of the pile of utensils.

Sure enough, the mistress saw him, just as he had hoped she would. She picked him up and looked at him in relief. Then she used him to take the cap off a bottle.

Bottle Opener did a good job. He took the cap off with one stroke. He felt very happy. He hadn't realized he was special and that's why he didn't get used as much as the other utensils. "I'll never feel useless again," he said to himself. "Now I know I was made for a special reason."

God has a special purpose for each one of us. It doesn't make any difference how little or unimportant we may feel; in God's sight we are very important.

33 A Special Job

Object: *A fishnet.*

Ron smiled as he tossed his fishing line into the water. He was going to have lots of fun. All week he had been looking forward to coming here to his grandfather's pond. Last Sunday he had learned that he and his folks were going to come, and ever since then he had anticipated this very moment.

He sat down on the bank to wait for the tiny jerk that would make his cork bob, indicating there was a fish on his hook.

It wasn't long until it happened. Down went the cork. Ron jerked his pole. He had it! He was sure he had it. Carefully he let the fish swim around a little. The tug on his bamboo pole told him the fish was a big one.

As he pulled the fish closer to the shore, Ron realized he had forgotten his net. He had been in such a hurry to get down to the pond he had forgotten it.

Quickly he tried to figure out a way to grab the fish when he got it up to the bank. But there wasn't anything near him that he could use. He could see a big can down a little way, but it was out of reach.

Ron did the best he could. He dragged the fish up on the bank and tried to grab it with his hands. But it was slippery and he couldn't get a good hold. The fish flopped back into the water.

Ron was disappointed, but he put another worm on his hook. Then he ran over to get the can so it would be handy when he caught another fish.

Again he tossed the line into the water and watched the cork settle. This time when he caught a fish he was going to be prepared.

Then he felt a gentle tug. The cork dipped. With a jerk, Ron hooked the fish. He had his can ready to catch the fish before it could flop back into the water.

Ron pushed the can under the fish. He was very careful to get it in just the right place. But quicker than a flash the fish was gone.

"Oh, no," he groaned. "Not again! There's no use fishing if I can't land one when I catch it."

Ron realized makeshift substitutes could never do the work of the fishnet. He'd just have to stop fishing for a little while and go up to the house and get it.

He ran all the way to the back porch where the net was lying, got it, and ran back to the pond. He grinned when he threw the line into the pond. This time he knew the fish would not get away!

Did you know that in one way you and I are like a fishnet? A fishnet is made for a specific job. You might be able to use it for a few other things, but it can't really do anything well except net fish.

God made you and me to serve Him in a particular way, too. He wants you to do some specific things for Him that nobody else can do. What do you think God wants you to do for Him? How can you find out what He wants you to do?

34 Each One of Us Is Special

Object: *A pair of scissors.*

The Bible tells us that God made us and has a plan for each of our lives. He even knew us before we were born! He made us as we are so we would be able to do what He wants us to do.

If you are a boy, you might look at some big, strong

boy and wish you were big and strong like him. Or, if you are a girl, you might look at some pretty girl and wish you were like her.

But did you know that God wants you to look just the way you do? He planned you before you were born. He planned the color of your hair, the color of your eyes, and the color of your skin. He planned whether you would be a boy or a girl. He even planned your nose size and how curly or straight your hair would be.

God made you the way He did because He wanted you to be special. Just like these scissors. The man who made them designed them so they would be able to do the job he wanted them to do. He didn't make these scissors so they could cut meat or draw a picture. He didn't make them to wash or eat with. He made them to cut material, string, ribbon, and paper.

Let's thank God for making us just the way we are, and for being special to Him.

11/20/94 **35 We All Have Labels**

Object: *A can of something.*

I have here in my hand a can of _____ . I know it is a can of _____ because of its label.

If I had a whole shelf full of unlabeled canned vegetables and fruit, I'd never know what each can contained until I opened it.

If I liked surprises that might be all right, but if I opened three different cans I might end up with three cans of the same thing. Or, I might want a variety of vegetables and fruit and end up with all vegetables or all fruit instead.

It would be just as bad, or worse, if all the labels on the cans weren't correct. Then I might plan a meal, thinking all the labels were correct, and end up with something entirely different from what I wanted.

Manufacturers are required to put labels on their cans and bottles. All the ingredients must be listed on these labels. If manufacturers don't do this, they are breaking a law.

We don't have our "ingredients" written on us, but people can see what kind of a person we are by the things we do and the way that we do them. God has given His people commandments to be obedient to Him. When we are obedient to those commandments, other people can see that we love Him.

36 Pictures Don't Lie

Object: *A photograph.*

There's an old saying, "pictures don't lie."

If somebody took a picture of you when you were a little baby, you can know now how you looked then. Somebody may recall that you were a chubby little baby. Someone else might remember you as being a bald baby. But if you have a picture of yourself, you can look at it to see exactly how you looked.

I have here a picture of _____ when he (she) was _____ years old. This picture shows us what _____ used to look like.

When somebody paints a picture, it doesn't show a person exactly as he is. But a photograph usually tells the truth.

God wants us all to be like a photograph. He wants us to tell the truth.

37 A Clean Sweep

Object: *A broom.*

Here is a broom. This broom's job is to clean up anything I want it to clean. When I want to sweep the kitchen, I take this broom to the kitchen, hold it in my hands like this, and sweep. (Illustrate.) I can also use this broom to sweep the sidewalk or the inside of my car.

This broom is a good broom. It does just what I want it to do. If I took it into the kitchen, out to the sidewalk, or out to the car and it refused to sweep, I wouldn't bother with it any more. Or, if it got all scraggly and the bristles fell out, I'd get rid of it. (Throw broom aside.)

A broom that doesn't do what I want it to do wouldn't

help me clean up anything. It would be a lot of trouble to handle and I'd never get the job done.

God has trouble with people sometimes. He tries to get them to do what He wants them to do, but sometimes He has to let them go their way and get into trouble.

In the Bible God tells us what He wants us to do and what He doesn't want us to do. If we love Him and want to obey Him, we will read our Bibles to find out what His commandments are. God has promised us a good, abundant life if we follow His commandments, and God always keeps His promises.

One more thing. God doesn't expect you to follow these commandments all by yourself. When you accept Jesus as your Savior, He comes into your heart and forgives you of your sins. Then, as you ask Him to help you follow Him, He will help you live a clean, holy life.

38 Praise God for Everything

Objects: *Paper towel and a cup of water.*

We have lots of things today that our grandparents and great-grandparents didn't have. Paper towels, for instance.

Let's pretend that I am the cup I am holding here in my hand. And let's pretend the paper towel is God and that the water in my cup is praise for God. If I want to let the paper towel (God) receive the water (my praise), I have to move my cup over to where the paper towel is.

If I have all the praise in the world in me and if I love God with all my heart, it won't do God one bit of good unless I give it to Him. But, if I take the praise to God (move the cup over to a position where the towel can begin to absorb some of the water), God receives it. He draws it up to Himself.

What does God do with praise? He changes it to blessings and then passes it right back to us! (Squeeze the water out of the towel back into the cup.) The wonderful thing about God is that He really isn't like this towel, because He gives us back much more than we give to Him.

Try praising God in all things this week—for both the good *and* the bad things that happen—and see how much He will bless you.

39 Jesus Makes Us Clean

Objects: *A dirty rag and a clean handkerchief.*

(Hold up dirty rag.) This rag is so dirty I can't get it clean. No matter how hard I scrub, or how often, it still looks dirty.

If we are very careful and don't get our clothes too

dirty, we can wash them and they will come out looking like this handkerchief, as good as new. (Show clean handkerchief.)

In a way, we are like rags and clean clothes. We get dirty. I'm not talking about the kind of dirt we get on our skins that we can wash off. I'm talking about the kind of dirt that gets inside of us. It is the bad thoughts and feelings and the things those bad thoughts and feelings get us to do.

God calls these bad things that we think and do "sin," and He tells us in the Bible that no one can come into His presence with sin. God is so pure and holy He cannot even look at sin.

We know everyone has sinned. God says so, and we know it, too, when we look at ourselves and others and see the things we and they do.

If everyone has sinned, how can any of us ever get to be with God? God has made a Way. He tells us that when we accept Jesus as our Savior He will never be able to see our sins because He will then be looking at us through Jesus.

If we accept Jesus as Savior, a new, clean spirit is born within us, and in God's sight we become clean and pure, like this handkerchief.

God tells us when we accept Jesus as our Savior that we will have eternal life. He will always be with us, even when we die. In fact, when we have Jesus in our hearts, we never really die. Our bodies will stop working some day, but our souls will go to be with Him.

I'm glad God made a Way so we don't have to be like this dirty old rag. I'm glad Jesus makes us clean, pure, and holy when we accept Him as our Savior.

40 God Wants Us to Do Something

Object: *A bar of soap.*

By the time we are four years old, we are big enough to be helpers. And the older we get the more responsibilities we are able to handle. You can keep your toys picked up, make your own beds, put your dirty clothes in the dirty-clothes basket and your clean clothes in the closet and drawers. You can even help your mother do the dishes and sweep the floor. There are a lot of things boys and girls can do to help at home.

You can help in Sunday school and children's church by picking papers up off the floor and keeping the chairs straight. You can help your teacher pass out the Sunday-school papers. You can help by listening, too, and not making any noise so others can hear.

I brought this bar of soap for our lesson this morning. This soap may sit unused on the sink in the kitchen. It may also sit on the basin or on the side of the tub in the bathroom. It may stay all wrapped up in a dark closet. But, as long as it does only these things, it really isn't of any use at all. It has to get in somebody's hands and *work*.

That's the way it is with us. God doesn't want us to play all the time. He doesn't want us sitting around all the time watching television, either. He wants us to *do something*!

How do we know what God wants us to do? We can learn His will by reading the Bible and by listening to other people who know Him. And, if we are Christians, we can listen to Jesus who is in our hearts.

Just as this soap needs to be put into somebody's hands so it can do what it's supposed to do, we need to put ourselves in God's hands and do what He wants us to do.

41 God Has a Plan

Object: *A flower (may be artificial).*

God has a plan for everything. He has a plan for animals, a plan for plants, and a plan for you.

God has given animals what we call instinct. He has arranged for them to know how to build a home, how to find food, and how to protect themselves.

God has put into plants the ability to grow from a seed into a mature plant, such as this flower. (Show flower.) Everything that makes a flower look like what God wants it to look like is inside a little seed! When that seed is planted, the flower grows up to be exactly what it should be. If it is a daisy seed, a daisy grows. If it is a marigold seed, a marigold grows.

Nature obeys God. If the animals and plants didn't do what they are supposed to do, everything would be quite mixed up.

God has a plan for us, too. He wants us to obey Him, but He doesn't treat us like plants and animals. We grow up to look like what God has made us to look like, but there is another part of us that is different from the rest of the world. We are made in God's image. He has given us the ability to make choices.

Some people want to follow God's plan and choose to obey Him; others choose not to obey God. When we choose to do what God wants us to do, we make Him happy, and we also make ourselves happy. I want to be happy, and I want God to be happy, too.

42 God Is Everywhere

Object: *A ceramic doll or figurine.*

God has always wanted His people to worship Him. But many times men, women, boys, and girls turn their backs on Him and worship other things.

Did you know that whatever you think about most is your god, and that is what you worship? The most important things in some people's lives are their cars, their houses, their dolls, or their bicycles. Some people even worship images or idols that actually look a bit like this doll!

We wonder how they can worship something man-made, something that can't breathe, move, or think. But they do. Sometimes Satan fools us so much we do foolish things.

We should be very grateful to God that we can read His Word and learn all about Him. We can't see God as we can see this doll, but that doesn't mean we can't worship Him. In fact, because God is a Spirit who can't be seen, it's possible for Him to be everywhere at the same time.

Isn't it wonderful to know that no matter where you are God is there, too? Because of this, we can worship Him anytime and anyplace.

You certainly couldn't worship this doll wherever you might happen to be, could you? You might forget it and leave it someplace. And, if you had it, as we said before, it wouldn't do you any good because this doll can't do anything anyway.

Why do you think God wants us to worship Him? God is very, very wise. He knows that if we keep our hearts and minds on Him we will be thinking about how great and wonderful He is. Then our problems will seem very small in comparison and it will be easy to give them to Him and trust Him to take care of us.

43 God Shares with Us

Object: *A book.*

Have you read a good book lately? I just finished reading this book. (Show book.) It is a good book with lots of ideas in it that I will share with my friends.

That's the way most people are. When we enjoy something, we like to share it. When we get a new tricycle or bicycle or dog or cat, we like to show it to our friends. Maybe that's because we are made in God's image. We know that God has always shared with mankind.

God shared the sun, the moon, and the stars with us. He shared the mountains and the oceans and everything that grows on the earth. He shared all the good things we have because every good thing we have comes to us from God.

But the greatest thing that God shared with us is His Son. If God had not shared Jesus and let Him come to the earth to die for our sins, God wouldn't have been able to share heaven with us. God loved us so much He was willing to share the most precious thing He had.

44 God Protects Us

Object: *Umbrella.*

An umbrella is a very handy article to have when it rains. (Show umbrella. Demonstrate how to use it.) When you open it up and hold it over your head, your head and shoulders remain dry. Of course, a raincoat and boots are necessary if you are to stay dry all over.

God wants us to make the best of what we have. He doesn't expect us to use something we don't have, but He does want us to use what we have. Like this umbrella. It would be pretty silly to walk down the street in pouring rain while carrying your umbrella under your arm. To be of any value, it has to be used.

God is like an umbrella in our lives. He is always with us and is always willing to help and protect us. All we have to do is to ask Him and let Him. Just as we "ask" the umbrella to open up by pushing in the little spring and pushing up the top.

Feel God's presence close to you and pray. You don't need to pray out loud. God knows what is in your mind. He knows everything and is everywhere. Remember the umbrella and how it protects you. And remember that God protects you and takes care of you. God loves you. He wants to help you, if you'll just let Him.

45 Worshiping God

Objects: *Bible, song book, collection plate (or church-offering envelope).*

God wants us to worship Him. We worship Him by telling Him how much we love Him and how wonderful we think He is. We can do this in several ways. We can worship by praying or by reading the Bible. (Show Bible.) We can worship Him by singing songs. (Show song book.) We can worship Him by giving Him money. (Show collection plate or church-offering envelope.)

But we can do these things without worshiping God

at all. We can pray, read our Bibles, sing, or even give money to Him without doing it in love. Worship must be from our hearts. We need to think about what we are saying and doing, and we need to be sincere and mean every word for it to be worship.

How can we read the Bible and not have it do us any good? This can happen because we sometimes read it without believing what God says in it. In order for the Bible to do any good, we must pay attention to it and believe what it says. If we read it lovingly and prayerfully, believing every word, we are worshiping.

We can pray and not pay any attention to what we are saying or think about God. That kind of prayer couldn't possibly be worship, could it?

We can give our money to God and not be worshiping. We give it to Him by putting it into an offering envelope or the collection plate. The money is used to help God's work, like paying bills in the church, and buying song books and Sunday-school papers. It is also used to send missionaries to other countries to teach people about God. The money we give can do all these things, but if we don't give it lovingly and willingly, we are not using it to worship God.

The people in the Old Testament worshiped God in these ways—praying, singing, giving money. But they worshiped in another way, too. God told them they must give offerings to Him by killing an animal, placing it on an altar, and burning it. This sacrifice was necessary because only blood could be used to cover the sins of the people. We don't do this today, because Jesus, the greatest sacrifice of all, gave His life for us. And because He was the greatest sacrifice of all, no other sacrifice needs to be made.

When we think about the sacrifice Jesus made for us,

we truly want to worship God. We begin to see how wonderful, mighty, and magnificent He is. When we think of God in this way, we are worshiping.

46 God Wants Us to Be Honest

Object: *Pennies in a small purse.*

These are pennies. (Show them.) I keep them in this little purse. If someone took them from me when I wasn't looking, or if someone took them from me without my permission, that would be stealing.

Everyone knows what stealing is, and we know that it is wrong. But some people go ahead and take things that don't belong to them anyway.

The Bible tells us we should never take anything that does not belong to us, unless the owner says it is all right. Today I am going to give my pennies away. (Give some or all the pennies to individual boys and girls.)

Now I am happy, because I shared. And you're happy because I shared, too. But you really wouldn't have been happy if you had taken that penny without my consent. You would have felt guilty and afraid that someone would find out what you had done.

If you had taken the penny and hidden it in your pocket, and if I had counted my pennies and found one missing, I might ask you about it. "Did you see one of my pennies? It is missing."

You could say, "Yes, I took it." But you probably wouldn't. You most likely would say, "No, I haven't seen it."

Now you not only have stolen the penny, you have lied about it.

God knows we feel good when we tell the truth. He knows that other people will trust us, too, if we tell the truth. God is honest and we can believe what He says. He wants us to be honest, too.

47 God Gives Us Our Families

Objects: *Knife, fork, and spoon.*

People in different parts of the world eat in different ways. There are some in New Guinea who don't use anything except their hands. Some people, like the Chinese, eat with chopsticks.

But we use these when we eat. (Show knife, fork, and spoon.) Each one of these utensils has a special purpose. We use the knife to cut meat. We use it to cut butter and to spread it on bread, corn on the cob, or baked potatoes. We use the fork for most of our eating. And for things we can't pick up with a fork, like soup and ice cream, we use a spoon.

Just as we need to have a knife, a fork, and a spoon because each has its special purpose, we need to have different members of a family.

The knife will represent the father. Fathers are very important to families. Fathers usually work hard so we can have enough money to pay the bills. They fix things for us and take care of us.

Let's let the fork stand for our mothers. Mothers are very important, too. They take care of the house and cook our meals. They wash and iron our clothes. Sometimes they have jobs to help pay for the bills, too. They do lots of things to make us happy and to make us feel good.

But to make a real set of silverware we need a spoon, too. Maybe even several spoons. Let's let this spoon represent you.

Sometimes boys and girls fuss and fight. God didn't make us so we would fuss and fight. He made us so we could help right where He put us. And that is right in our homes. We can help by picking up our toys and clothes. Each one of us has a special place to fill at home.

It doesn't make any difference how many boys and girls are in a family. Mother and father love each one the same. And we know God loves each one of us the same, too.

Let's thank God right now for our families. For father and mother and for each brother and sister. Let's thank Him that He has put us in our particular family because that is where He knows we should be.

48 Following God

Objects: *Needle and thread.*

How many of you can sew? Sewing is very important for us. Someone has to sew so we can have clothes to wear. Often someone needs to sew to keep our clothes in good condition so we can wear them.

What do we need to sew patches on blue jeans? Yes, a needle and thread. (Show needle and thread. Do not have the needle threaded.) The needle would not be able to do anything at all if it were used all alone. The thread couldn't do anything by itself, either. You have to have a needle in order to get the thread through the material.

Here we have both the needle and the thread, but neither can do any good alone. So, we thread the needle. (Thread it.) Now the needle can go into the material, as it's supposed to. And the thread can get into the material by following the needle.

God wants us to follow Him just as thread follows the needle. Alone we can do nothing, but with God leading us we can do what we are supposed to do.

How do we know what God wants us to do? By talking to Him and by listening to what He has to say to us.

We can also read our Bibles. The Bible is God's Word. It is God talking to us. He had men write down all the things He wanted us to know, but we must read the Bible if it is going to do us any good.

Sometimes we may not understand what the Bible says, but there are many things we can understand. We can read those things and do them until we grow a little and are able to understand more and more.

If we want to follow God, like this thread following the needle, we can. Then we will do what we are supposed to do. We will be happy because we are being obedient to God.

4/14/96

49 Working Together with God

Objects: *Hammer and nail.*

Here is a hammer and nail. (Show them.) Hammers and nails come in very handy. Especially when you want to build a house or repair a cupboard.

This hammer is a good hammer. It is the right shape and size. It weighs as much as a hammer should weigh. However, there are not many uses for it unless it has some nails to pound.

A hammer and nail work together like a needle and thread. A nail needs a hammer to pound it into place. Take a nail that you want to hang a picture on, for instance. This nail is a good strong nail, but I can't press it into the wall. I can't pound it in with my fist, either. Even if I could, that would hurt my hand. You can't pound the wall with the hammer, either. You would only knock down all the plaster and ruin the wall!

But, when you use the hammer to pound the nail into the wall, you not only don't mess the wall up, you have something to hang your picture on.

We need to be like nails. They are willing to do what the hammer wants them to do. We need to be willing to do what God wants us to do.

You can read your Bible and talk to grown-ups who can help you find out what God is saying to you. Even after you find out what God is saying, it isn't always easy to do; but God will help you as the hammer helps the nail.

For instance, if some friends of yours are teasing a new boy in the neighborhood, it may not be easy to say, "No, that's not right. I'm not going to tease him." God says to love one another, and you certainly aren't loving someone if you are teasing him. If you work with God, He will help you do the right thing.

50 Friends

Object: *Long jump-rope.*

God knows that we need friends, so He has built within us a desire to make friends and to be a friend. Of course, He is our best Friend. We know this because He loved us so much He wanted us to be with Him forever. He made this possible by sending His Son, Jesus, to live on the earth.

If God had not loved us so much, Jesus would have stayed in His beautiful heavenly home and not bothered to do all He did for us. Jesus gave up that wonderful home so we can live with Him forever. It would not have been possible for us to go to heaven to be with Him if He had not made a way for us. That makes Him our very best Friend.

God wants us to have friends on earth, too. We know this because He gave us language so we can talk and play with each other. We can help each other, too.

I have a long jump-rope here. (Show rope.) Most boys and girls like to jump rope. If you have a short rope or if you double up a long rope, you can jump by yourself. But it's a lot more fun to jump with our friends. To jump with this long rope, it takes three people. One on each end to hold the rope and one in the middle to jump. (Allow three children to demonstrate.)

God is good to give us friends. He is good to let us be a friend, too. But, best of all, it is good to know that He is our very best Friend.

51 God Wants Us to Worship Him

Object: *A chair.*

Do you see this empty chair? (Put chair on the platform.) It is empty today because someone is absent. Do you know somebody who isn't here who could have been here if you had invited him? (Let children name some people.)

God wants us to come to church every Sunday to worship Him, and He wants us to invite others, too. In Hebrews 10:25 God tells us to get together with other people who love Him so we can worship Him together.

What is worship? (Allow response.) It is praying, singing, giving our money, and listening to someone talk about God. It is thinking about God and loving Him very much and telling Him so.

This empty chair represents someone who did not come today. Whoever it is did not get to worship God today. I hope that you won't ever leave an empty chair in church because you are not here when you could have been. It always pleases God when we love Him enough to come to His house to worship Him.

52 New Year's Resolutions (New Year)

Objects: *Calendar for the past and current years.*

Look! (Show old calendar.) This calendar represents a whole year in your life! In just a short time these months have gone. You will never be able to live them again.

January is gone. (Turn page, and keep turning them.) February is gone. March, April, May. All of them are gone, except for the memory we have of them, and the consequences of what we have done in them.

Sometimes we feel sad because time has passed and we haven't used it well. I think this is true of grown-ups more than boys and girls, but boys and girls can feel this way, too.

Are you pleased with the way you spent your time last year? Are you pleased with all the grades you made in school? Are you pleased with how you have treated your friends and your parents? Are you satisfied with the way you have treated God?

If you are like most people, and if you are honest, you'll probably have to admit you didn't do so well in everything last year.

Maybe your grades weren't as good as they could have been, or you weren't as nice to your friends and parents as you could have been. Maybe you didn't really talk to God much, or let Him talk to you.

It's a good thing to look back on the old year, because we can do something about it. First, we can check ourselves out to see how and what we've been doing. Then we can ask God to forgive us for those things we've done that have not been pleasing to Him.

We can ask our teachers, friends, and parents to forgive us if we have done something that needs to be forgiven. And then, of course, we must forgive ourselves.

We can prove we really mean what we are saying by asking God to help us do better in the new year. (Show new calendar.) Every page is still clean in this new year. We have a choice to do what we will with each new day.

(Spend some time talking about the past year and the new year. Pray together asking for forgiveness from God for past failures and for help to do better in the future. Be sure to explain God forgives all year long, not just on New Year's.)

53 God's Valentine (Valentine's Day)

Objects: *A valentine and a Bible.*

Valentine's Day is a very special day. We look forward to it for a long time because it is a day that makes us happy.

Sometimes we start two weeks early to get all our valentines ready to give to our friends and loved ones. And we look forward to receiving valentines, too.

Valentines come in all sizes. There are big ones and little ones and middle-sized ones. I brought one with me. (Show valentine, leaving it standing on a table.)

Although some people like to send funny valentines to make people laugh, most of us send pretty valentines to tell other people how much we love them. We send them to our friends in school and church, our parents, our grandparents, our aunts and uncles, and our teachers.

Valentine's Day is one day a year that people have set aside to send greetings of love.

Do you know that God has sent a valentine to you? He has! Do you know that to God every day is Valentine's Day?

Can you guess what God's valentine is? Let me give you some hints. (Give the hints until someone guesses that the Bible is God's valentine.)

(1) It tells us how much God loves us. (2) It tells us all about God's love-gift, Jesus. (3) It comes in two parts. (4) It has sixty-six books in it.

Yes, the Bible is God's love letter to us. (Place the Bible beside the valentine.)

So remember, if you don't receive any valentines from your friends this year, you still have received the biggest and best valentine in the whole world. It is from your best Friend who loves you very, very much!

54 The Cross Is Empty! (Easter)

Object: *A cross.*

Easter is a time when we celebrate new life. It is the special time of year when we remember Jesus and all He has done for us. It is the time of year when we thank Him for dying on the cross for us. But, above all, it is the time of year when we rejoice because Jesus didn't stay dead. Three days later, He was alive, walking and talking with people!

At Easter we celebrate spring and the coming back to life of all the flowers, grass, and trees. We celebrate by having new clothes and Easter eggs. The new clothes remind of us of new life, and so do the eggs.

But today I want to talk about this cross. (Show the cross.) I want to talk about the *empty* cross.

Some people think that Jesus' life ended when he died on the cross. In fact, they have pictures and crucifixes with Him on the cross. But, praise the Lord! The cross is empty!

Jesus died for us. He paid the price for our salvation.

He took the punishment for our sins. We thank Him so much. He made it possible for us to live with Him forever!

Every time you see a cross, remember that Jesus died on a cross. Remember, too, that now He is alive! The cross is empty!

55 On Being Thankful (Thanksgiving)

Object: *A bowl of fruit.*

Thanksgiving Day is a special day to the people in our country. It is a holiday set aside for us to remember all the blessings God has given us.

The Pilgrims celebrated the first Thanksgiving because they wanted God to know how much they appreciated letting them come to a new country where they could be free to worship Him. They wanted to thank Him, too, for saving their lives and for giving them crops so they could have food to eat.

Those Pilgrims had many hardships, but they didn't complain because of them. No! They worked hard, prayed hard, and trusted God.

They could have grumbled because the work had been so hard and because they were cold and their lives had been threatened. They could have complained because of the loss of so many of their loved ones. But they believed in God. They trusted Him and they were grateful for what they had.

The fruit in this bowl (show fruit) represents the big banquet the Pilgrims had on their first Thanksgiving Day. It also represents the seeds that the Pilgrims sowed, the ground they cultivated, and the fruits and vegetables that finally grew. It represents how God provided for them because of their labor. It shows how God answers prayers.

Most importantly, this fruit can remind us to be thankful in all things. God wants us to be thankful when good things happen to us, of course, but He also wants us to be thankful when bad things happen.

Do you know why? Because when we are thankful to Him we are opening ourselves up to His blessings, and showing Him we trust Him in all things. When we are thankful He can show us that good can come out of even the bad.

Let's remember to thank God in all things as the Pilgrims did. Let's make every day a Thanksgiving Day.

56 God Takes Care of Us (Christmas)

Object: *A Christmas tree ornament.*

Everybody loves Christmas trees. Christmas trees are beautiful and colorful and they make everyone happy. Some Christmas trees are white, some are silver, some are green. But it doesn't make any difference what color a Christmas tree is—to be a real Christmas tree, ornaments have to be hanging from its branches. (Show ornament.)

Nearly every family has old-fashioned ornaments stored away, all wrapped up in white tissue paper and packed in a box. We take them out every year and place them very carefully on the branches of the tree. We wouldn't want to break them because these ornaments are very precious. Every time you see them they remind you of all the happy times you've had on Christmas.

Maybe some day when you grow up you will have on your Christmas tree some of the same beautiful ornaments that you have right now. And you can, if you take good care of them!

God made the world and everything in it. When He made all these things, He didn't forget them. He takes very good care of all His creation. Sometimes people cause problems for Him, but He still takes care of everything He has made.